PUGLIA TRAVEL GUIDE

Puglia Unveiled: A Journey through the Sun Drenched Jewel of Italy

Jerry Chavis

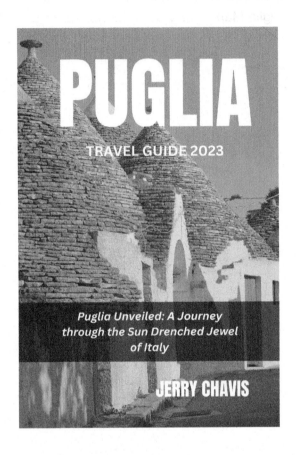

CHAPTER 1: INTRODUCTION TO PUGLIA

Once upon a time, in the enchanting land of Italy, nestled along the picturesque coastline of the Adriatic Sea, lay a hidden gem awaiting discovery. Its name was Puglia, a region steeped in ancient history, breathtaking landscapes, and a rich tapestry of cultural treasures. From the moment travelers set foot upon its sun-kissed shores, they were transported into a world where time seemed to stand still, and every experience was filled with wonder.

Puglia, also known as Apulia, was a land of contrasts. Its rugged coastline stretched for miles, adorned with dramatic cliffs that plunged into crystal-clear turquoise waters. Here, visitors could bask in the warmth of the Mediterranean sun, feeling the gentle sea breeze caress their skin as they explored secluded coves and pristine beaches. The Adriatic Sea whispered stories of sailors and merchants who had traversed its waters for centuries, leaving behind a legacy of maritime adventures and seafaring traditions.

As travelers ventured further inland, they discovered a land teeming with fertile valleys and endless olive groves, earning Puglia its reputation as the "Garden of Italy." Rolling hills dotted with charming whitewashed villages and ancient vineyards embraced visitors, inviting them to indulge in the region's famed gastronomic delights. Puglia's culinary heritage was an irresistible blend of flavors, drawing inspiration from its Mediterranean roots. Plates overflowed with luscious tomatoes, fragrant basil, and velvety olive oil, accompanied by freshly caught seafood and handmade pasta.

Every corner of Puglia told a story of its past, where ancient civilizations had left their indelible mark. The trulli, traditional cone-shaped houses with whitewashed walls and distinctive conical roofs, stood as architectural marvels, a testament to the region's unique heritage. In Alberobello, a UNESCO World Heritage Site, rows of trulli created a fairytale-like setting, transporting visitors back in time to a bygone era.

Puglia's cities were vibrant and lively, blending old-world charm with modern delights. Bari, the capital, bustled with life, its labyrinthine streets leading to stunning cathedrals and bustling markets. Lecce, known as the "Florence of the South," mesmerized visitors with its intricate Baroque architecture, adorned with ornate carvings and delicate lace-like stonework.

Throughout the year, Puglia embraced its vibrant culture with colorful festivals and lively celebrations. From the rhythmic tarantella dances to the captivating sounds of traditional folk music, the region's soul resonated with joy and a deep sense of community. Visitors were welcomed with open arms, invited to join in the revelry and create cherished memories that would last a lifetime.

As the sun set over Puglia's rolling hills, casting a warm golden glow upon its ancient ruins and enchanting landscapes, travelers felt a deep sense of gratitude for having embarked on this unforgettable journey. Puglia had captured their hearts, igniting a passion for exploration and a yearning to delve deeper into the wonders of this magical region.

And so, with each passing day, Puglia continued to inspire, delight, and beckon travelers from far and wide to uncover its hidden treasures. With a travel guide in hand, adventurers set forth, ready to immerse themselves in the splendor of Puglia, where ancient tales intertwined with modern enchantment, creating an experience beyond compare.

1.1 Geography And Location

Puglia, also known as Apulia in English, is a region located in the southern part of Italy. It is situated on the Adriatic Sea, with a long coastline stretching approximately 800 kilometers (500 miles). Puglia occupies the "heel" of Italy's boot-shaped peninsula and is bordered by the regions of Molise and Campania to the west, Basilicata to the southwest, and the Adriatic Sea to the east.

Geographically, Puglia is characterized by diverse landscapes that range from stunning coastal areas to rolling hills, fertile plains, and rugged mountainous terrain. The region covers an area of about 19,358 square kilometers (7,469 square miles), making it the sixth-largest region in Italy.

Puglia's coastline is one of its most prominent features, offering beautiful beaches, picturesque cliffs, and charming fishing villages. The most famous coastal areas in Puglia include the Gargano Peninsula, which forms the spur of Italy's boot, and the Salento Peninsula, which forms the heel. These areas are renowned for their crystal-clear waters, sandy beaches, and rocky coves.

Moving inland, Puglia's landscape transforms into a mix of fertile plains and gently rolling hills. This region is often referred to as the "breadbasket of Italy" due to its agricultural significance. Puglia is known for its extensive olive groves, vineyards, and fields of wheat. The region produces a significant portion of Italy's olive oil and wine.

The central part of Puglia is characterized by the Murge Plateau, a vast limestone plateau dotted with charming villages and historic towns. This area features a unique karst landscape with sinkholes, caves, and underground rivers. The Murge Plateau is known for its agricultural productivity, particularly in the cultivation of cereals, almonds, and cherries.

To the west of the Murge Plateau, Puglia is bordered by the rugged and mountainous terrain of the Gargano Promontory. This area is home to the Gargano National Park, which encompasses forests, lakes, and dramatic coastal cliffs. The Gargano Promontory is a popular destination for outdoor enthusiasts, offering opportunities for hiking, mountain biking, and wildlife observation.

In terms of climate, Puglia experiences a Mediterranean climate, characterized by hot and dry summers, mild winters, and a high number of sunshine hours throughout the year. However, there can be regional variations within the area due to its diverse geography.

In summary, Puglia is a captivating region in southern Italy that boasts a stunning coastline, picturesque countryside, and a rich agricultural heritage. Its diverse geography, ranging from coastal areas to fertile plains and rugged mountains, contributes to its unique charm and appeal.

1.2 Climate And Weather

Puglia, also known as Apulia, is a region located in southern Italy, characterized by a Mediterranean climate. The region experiences mild, wet winters and hot, dry summers, typical of Mediterranean regions. The climate in Puglia is influenced by its proximity to the Adriatic Sea and the Ionian Sea, which moderate temperatures and create a pleasant coastal environment. Below are the weather patterns in Puglia:

Seasons:

Spring (March to May): Spring in Puglia is mild and pleasant, with gradually increasing temperatures. Average temperatures range from 10°C (50°F) in March to 20°C (68°F) in May. The region experiences moderate rainfall during this season, contributing to the blossoming of flowers and vegetation.

Summer (June to August): Summers in Puglia are hot and dry, with plenty of sunshine. Average temperatures range from 24°C (75°F) in June to 30°C (86°F) in August, occasionally reaching higher temperatures. This is the peak tourist season in Puglia due to the warm weather and the vibrant beach atmosphere.

Autumn (September to November):

Autumn in Puglia is mild and pleasant, with decreasing temperatures. Average temperatures range from 22°C (72°F) in September to 14°C (57°F) in November. The rainfall increases during this season, particularly in November, but it is still relatively lower compared to other parts of Italy.

Winter (December to February): Puglia experiences mild winters with cool temperatures. Average temperatures range from 12°C (54°F) in December to 8°C (46°F) in February. While it can be chilly, snowfall is rare in most parts of the region, except in higher elevations. Winter is the wettest season in Puglia, with occasional rainfall and some windy days.

Precipitation:

Puglia receives most of its rainfall between October and March, with November being the wettest month. The region generally experiences a Mediterranean pattern of rainfall, characterized by short, intense showers. The average annual precipitation ranges from 500 to 700 millimeters (20 to 28 inches), with coastal areas receiving slightly less rainfall than the inland areas.

Winds:

Puglia is influenced by various winds that affect its climate. The most notable is the Scirocco, a hot and dry wind that blows from the southeast, carrying desert dust from North Africa. The Scirocco can cause temporary increases in temperature and reduced visibility. The region also experiences the Mistral, a cold, northwesterly wind that brings cooler air during the summer months, providing relief from the heat.

Coastal and Inland Differences:

Puglia's climate varies slightly between the coastal and inland areas. The coastal regions experience a more temperate climate due to the moderating influence of the sea, with slightly milder winters and cooler summers compared to the inland areas. The coastal regions also tend to have a higher level of humidity.

In summary, Puglia enjoys a Mediterranean climate characterized by mild, wet winters and hot, dry summers. The region is known for its long, sunny days, making it an attractive destination for tourists seeking a beach holiday. However, it's important to note that weather patterns can vary from year to year, so it's always advisable to check the local forecast for the most accurate and up-to-date information before planning a trip.

1.3 Cultural Background

Puglia is characterized by its rich cultural heritage, which is a result of the region's history and influences from various civilizations that have inhabited the area throughout the centuries.

Historically, Puglia was inhabited by the Messapians, an ancient Italic tribe. Later, it was colonized by the Greeks, who established important city states such as Taranto and Brindisi. The Greek influence can still be seen today in the region's architecture, art, and even cuisine.

During the Roman period, Puglia became an important agricultural region, known for its production of olive oil and wine. The Romans constructed numerous villas, theaters, and aqueducts, many of which can still be visited today.

In the Middle Ages, Puglia experienced various invasions and dominations. The Byzantines, Lombards, Normans, and Swabians all left their mark on the region. The Norman period, in particular, had a significant impact on the culture of Puglia. The Normans built stunning cathedrals and castles, blending Byzantine, Arab, and Romanesque architectural styles.

During the Renaissance, Puglia saw a flourishing of art and culture. The city of Lecce became known as the "Florence of the South" due to its magnificent Baroque architecture. The region's cities and towns feature beautiful palaces, churches, and sculptures that reflect this artistic period.

Puglia has also been influenced by its geographic location, as it has been a crossroads of different cultures throughout history. Its position on the Adriatic and Ionian Seas made it a hub for trade and cultural exchange. It has been influenced by the Arabs, who brought their architectural styles and introduced new agricultural techniques. Puglia was also part of the Kingdom of Naples and later the Kingdom of Italy, which brought further influences and cultural integration.

One of the most prominent aspects of Puglia's culture is its cuisine. The region is known for its simple yet flavorful dishes, often based on local ingredients such as olive oil, tomatoes, seafood, and vegetables. Puglia is famous for its pasta, including orecchiette, a small ear-shaped pasta, and the traditional dish "orecchiette con le cime di rapa" (orecchiette with turnip tops). The region is also renowned for its wines, especially Primitivo and Negroamaro.

Folk traditions and festivals play a significant role in Puglia's cultural fabric. The Taranta Festival, held in various towns during the summer, celebrates traditional music and dance, particularly the famous Tarantella. These festivities reflect the region's lively and joyful spirit.

In recent years, Puglia has gained popularity as a tourist destination, attracting visitors with its picturesque landscapes, charming towns, and beautiful coastline. The region's cultural heritage, combined with its warm hospitality and delicious cuisine, makes it a unique and captivating place to explore.

CHAPTER 2: PLANNING YOUR TRIP TO PUGLIA

2.1 Best Time To Visit

The best time to visit Puglia largely depends on your preferences, as the region offers something unique throughout the year:

Spring (March to May):
Spring is a delightful time to visit Puglia. The weather starts to warm up, with temperatures ranging from 15°C (59°F) to 25°C (77°F) during the day. The landscape bursts into colorful blooms, and the countryside becomes vibrant with wildflowers. It's a perfect time for nature walks, exploring the charming villages, and enjoying outdoor activities. The tourist crowds are relatively smaller

compared to the peak summer season, making it a great time for a more relaxed experience. However, keep in mind that the evenings can still be cool, so packing some light jackets or sweaters is advisable.

Summer (June to August):

Summer is the peak tourist season in Puglia, and for good reason. The weather is hot and sunny, with temperatures ranging from 25°C (77°F) to 35°C (95°F) or even higher. The crystal-clear waters of the Adriatic and Ionian Seas are perfect for swimming, sunbathing, and water sports. The coastal towns and beaches come alive with vibrant energy, and you can enjoy lively festivals, open-air concerts, and outdoor dining. However, it's worth noting that summer is also the busiest and most crowded time, especially in August when Italians go on their summer holidays. Booking accommodations and popular attractions in advance is recommended.

Autumn (September to November):
Autumn in Puglia is another wonderful time to visit. The weather remains warm and pleasant during September, with temperatures similar to those in spring. As the season progresses, the temperatures start to cool down, ranging from 15°C (59°F) to 25°C (77°F) in October and November. The summer crowds thin out, making it an ideal time to explore Puglia's picturesque towns, indulge in the region's culinary delights, and take leisurely walks through the countryside. Autumn also brings the grape harvest season, offering opportunities to visit vineyards and participate in wine tours. It's worth checking the specific dates for local food and wine festivals, as they are popular during this season.

Winter (December to February):

Winter in Puglia is relatively mild, with temperatures ranging from 8°C (46°F) to 15°C (59°F) during the day. While the region experiences occasional rainfall, it's generally less crowded, and you can enjoy a quieter and more authentic experience. The winter months are perfect for exploring Puglia's rich history and cultural heritage, as well as visiting historical sites such as Alberobello, Lecce, and Matera. Additionally, Puglia's cuisine shines during this season, with hearty traditional dishes like orecchiette pasta and slow-cooked meat stews being popular choices. It's important to note that some tourist attractions, restaurants, and hotels may have reduced hours or be temporarily closed during the winter, so it's advisable to plan accordingly.

In summary, the best time to visit Puglia depends on your preferences. Spring and autumn offer pleasant weather, smaller crowds, and opportunities to explore the region's natural beauty and cultural heritage. Summer is perfect for beach lovers and those who enjoy a lively atmosphere, while winter provides a quieter experience with a focus on history, local cuisine, and authentic charm. Ultimately, Puglia has something to offer year-round, so choose the time that aligns with your interests and enjoy the unique experiences the region

2.2 Duration of Stay

When planning a trip to Puglia, it's important to consider the duration of your stay to make the most of your experience.

The ideal duration of stay in Puglia largely depends on your interests, preferences, and the places you wish to visit. However, a recommended duration for a fulfilling visit to Puglia would be around one to two weeks. This time frame allows you to explore the region thoroughly and immerse yourself in its unique culture.

During your stay in Puglia, you can discover the magnificent trulli houses in Alberobello, a UNESCO World Heritage site, and wander through the narrow streets of Ostuni, often referred to as the "White City" due to its whitewashed buildings. You can also visit the enchanting coastal towns of Polignano a Mare and Monopoli, known for their breathtaking views, crystal-clear waters, and charming atmosphere.

The region's capital, Bari, is another must-visit destination, offering a fascinating blend of history, modernity, and vibrant street life. The historic center, known as Bari Vecchia, is a maze of narrow alleys and picturesque squares, where you can explore the Basilica di San Nicola, a significant pilgrimage site, and enjoy traditional local cuisine in the cozy restaurants.

If you're interested in exploring Puglia's natural beauty, make sure to visit the Gargano Peninsula, also known as the "Spur of Italy's Boot." This area is home to the stunning Gargano National Park, featuring breathtaking landscapes, pristine beaches, and the iconic Tremiti Islands.

Puglia is also renowned for its culinary delights, and food lovers will find themselves indulging in delicious dishes throughout their stay. Don't miss the opportunity to try local specialties such as orecchiette pasta, burrata cheese, seafood dishes, and the region's famous olive oil and wine.

To truly immerse yourself in the Puglian lifestyle and experience everything the region has to offer, a longer stay of two weeks or more is recommended. This will allow you to venture further into the countryside, explore hidden gems, and relax on the beautiful beaches. You can also take day trips to nearby regions such as Matera in Basilicata or the stunning Amalfi Coast.

In conclusion, the duration of your stay in Puglia depends on your personal preferences and the experiences you wish to have. However, to fully appreciate the beauty, history, culture, and cuisine of this remarkable region, a minimum stay of one to two weeks is recommended. Whether you choose to spend a shorter or longer period, Puglia is sure to captivate you with its enchanting charm and leave you with unforgettable memories.

2.3 Transportation Options

Puglia offers a range of transportation options for visitors to explore its picturesque landscapes, charming towns, and stunning coastline. Whether you prefer to travel by air, train, car, or public transportation, Puglia provides convenient and efficient ways to get around the region.

Air Travel:
Puglia is served by several airports, with the two main ones being Bari Karol Wojtyła Airport and Brindisi-Salento Airport. These airports connect Puglia to various domestic and international destinations. Travelers can find direct flights to major European cities, making it easily accessible for international visitors. From the airports, you can rent a car, take a taxi, or use public

transportation to reach your desired destination within Puglia.

Train:

The Italian rail network provides a reliable and efficient way to travel within Puglia. The primary train operator in Italy is Trenitalia. Puglia is well-connected by rail, with Bari and Lecce being the main railway hubs. Trains run regularly between major cities such as Bari, Brindisi, Lecce, Taranto, and Foggia, as well as smaller towns. The train system allows you to enjoy scenic views of the countryside while reaching your destination comfortably.

Car Rental:

Renting a car is a popular option for exploring Puglia, as it provides flexibility and convenience, especially for those who want to visit smaller towns and remote areas. Several car rental companies operate at airports, train stations, and major cities in Puglia. It's important to note that driving in the historic centers of towns can be challenging due to narrow streets and limited parking options. However, Puglia has well-maintained highways and roads, making it relatively easy to navigate between cities and attractions.

Public Transportation:

Puglia has an extensive public transportation network, including buses and regional trains. Local buses are a cost-effective way to travel within cities and towns, with routes connecting various neighborhoods and tourist spots. The regional train service, known as the Ferrovie del Sud Est, offers connections between smaller towns and rural areas. It's worth checking the schedules in advance, as they may vary depending on the season and day of the week.

Cycling and Walking:

Puglia's flat terrain and scenic landscapes make it an excellent region for cycling and walking enthusiasts. Many towns provide bike rental services, allowing visitors to explore at their own pace. Additionally, Puglia offers well-marked hiking trails, such as the Gargano National Park and the Salento Peninsula, which allow you to experience the region's natural beauty up close.

Overall, Puglia offers a variety of transportation options that cater to different preferences and budgets. Whether you prefer the convenience of flying, the flexibility of renting a car, or the affordability of public transportation, you can easily navigate and explore the captivating sights and flavors of this enchanting region in southern Italy.

2.4 Visa And Entry Requirements

Visa Requirements for Puglia, Italy:
Puglia is a region located in Italy, and since Puglia is part of Italy, the visa requirements for Puglia are the same as those for Italy as a whole. Italy is a member of the Schengen Area, which is a group of European countries that have abolished passport control at their mutual borders. Therefore, if you are a citizen of a country that is part of the Schengen Area, you generally do not need a visa to enter Puglia or any other part of Italy.

Citizens of the European Union (EU) and the European Free Trade Association (EFTA) member states (such as Iceland, Liechtenstein, Norway, and Switzerland) can enter Italy with a valid national identity card or passport and stay for an unlimited period.

For citizens of other countries, including the United States, Canada, Australia, and many others, who are not part of the Schengen Area, a Schengen visa is generally required to enter Italy. The Schengen visa allows visitors to stay in Italy and the other Schengen countries for up to 90 days within a 180-day period.

It's important to note that visa requirements and exemptions can vary depending on the purpose of your visit, such as tourism, business, study, or work. If you are planning to stay in Puglia for a longer period or for purposes other than tourism, you may need to apply for a specific visa or permit.

Entry Requirements:

Regardless of whether you need a visa or not, there are some general entry requirements for visiting Puglia or any other part of Italy. These include:

Valid Passport: Your passport should be valid for at least six months beyond your intended stay in Italy.

Return Ticket: It's recommended to have a return ticket or proof of onward travel to demonstrate your intention to leave Italy within the allowed period.

Sufficient Funds: You may be asked to provide evidence of sufficient funds to cover your stay in Italy, such as bank statements or credit cards.

Accommodation: It's a good practice to have proof of accommodation arrangements for your stay in Puglia, such as hotel reservations or an invitation from a host.

Travel Insurance: While not mandatory, it is advisable to have travel insurance that covers medical expenses and repatriation in case of an emergency.

Additional Documents: Depending on your purpose of visit, you might be required to provide additional documents such as a letter of invitation, proof of employment, or enrollment in a study program.

It is always recommended to verify the most recent visa and entry requirements through official government sources, such as the website of the Italian Embassy or Consulate in your country.

2.5 Currency And Money Matters

When it comes to currency and money matters in Puglia, it operates within the framework of the Italian financial system and utilizes the euro (€) as its official currency.

The euro is the common currency of the European Union and is widely accepted throughout Puglia. It is divided into cents, with coins available in denominations of 1, 2, 5, 10, 20, and 50 cents, as well as 1 and 2 euro coins. Banknotes come in denominations of 5, 10, 20, 50, 100, 200, and 500 euros. Cash is widely used for daily transactions, especially in smaller establishments, although credit and debit cards are also widely accepted in most places, including hotels, restaurants, and larger stores.

It is advisable to carry some cash with you, especially when visiting smaller towns or rural areas where card acceptance may be limited. ATMs (Bancomat in Italian) are widely available in cities and towns, offering the convenience of withdrawing euros using international credit and debit cards. However, it's essential to notify your bank or financial institution before your trip to ensure that your card can be used in Italy and to inquire about any potential fees or restrictions.

Currency exchange services can be found at airports, banks, and some hotels. It's important to be cautious of exchange rates and any associated fees when exchanging money. Generally, using ATMs for cash withdrawal is considered a convenient and cost-effective option. However, it is recommended to compare rates and fees to find the best option for your specific needs.

In larger cities and popular tourist areas of Puglia, you will find a wide range of foreign exchange bureaus that offer currency exchange services. These establishments usually provide competitive rates, but it's always a good idea to compare rates and inquire about any fees before making the exchange.

When it comes to tipping, it is customary in Puglia to leave a small gratuity, particularly in restaurants and cafes. Tipping around 5-10% of the total bill is generally considered appropriate, but it's always at your discretion, based on the quality of service received.

In summary, Puglia operates within the eurozone, and the euro is the official currency. Cash is widely accepted, especially in smaller establishments, while credit and debit cards are commonly used. It's advisable to carry some cash, be mindful of any associated fees when using ATMs or exchanging currency, and inform your bank before your trip. By keeping these factors in mind, you can navigate currency and money matters in Puglia with ease during your visit to this beautiful region of Italy.

CHAPTER 3: EXPLORING THE CITIES AND TOWNS

3.1 Bari

Bari, located in the region of Puglia in southern Italy, is a vibrant city with a rich history, stunning architecture, and a captivating culture. Exploring Bari offers a wonderful opportunity to delve into the unique characteristics of this coastal city. Here are some of the reasons why Bari is worth exploring:

Historical Significance: Bari boasts a fascinating history that dates back to ancient times. It was a crucial port city during the Roman Empire and later became an important trading center in the Mediterranean. The city's historical significance is evident in its well-preserved landmarks and archaeological sites.

Bari Vecchia (Old Town): The heart of Bari is its captivating Old Town, known as Bari Vecchia. This medieval quarter is a maze of narrow winding streets, atmospheric squares, and whitewashed buildings adorned with colorful shutters. Walking through Bari Vecchia feels like stepping back in time, and it's a delight to explore the charming alleyways, visit historic churches, and stumble upon hidden treasures.

Basilica di San Nicola: Bari is famous for being the resting place of Saint Nicholas, the inspiration for Santa Claus. The Basilica di San Nicola is a prominent pilgrimage site and an architectural gem. This impressive Romanesque church houses the relics of Saint Nicholas and features stunning Byzantine-style mosaics, intricate carvings, and a serene atmosphere.

Castello Svevo (Swabian Castle): Situated on the waterfront, Castello Svevo is a formidable fortress that dates back to the 12th century. This well-preserved castle offers panoramic views of the city and the Adriatic Sea. Inside, you can explore the castle's rooms, visit the museum showcasing medieval artifacts, and learn about the city's history.

Bari Cathedral: The Cathedral of San Sabino is another must-visit attraction in Bari. This grand cathedral blends architectural styles from different periods, including Romanesque, Gothic, and Baroque. The interior is adorned with beautiful artworks, sculptures, and a stunning crypt that holds the remains of early Christian martyrs.

Seafront Promenade: Bari is a coastal city, and a stroll along the seafront promenade is a delightful experience. The Lungomare Nazario Sauro offers picturesque views of the Adriatic Sea, a refreshing sea breeze, and a lively atmosphere. You can find charming cafes, gelaterias, and seafood restaurants where you can savor the local cuisine.

Cuisine and Street Food: Bari is renowned for its mouthwatering cuisine and delectable street food. The city is famous for its fresh seafood, handmade pasta (such as orecchiette), and local specialties like the tiella (a savory rice, potato, and mussel dish) and focaccia barese (a traditional flatbread). Exploring the local markets and street food stalls is a fantastic way to immerse yourself in Bari's culinary delights.

Cultural Events: Bari hosts various cultural events throughout the year, providing visitors with a chance to experience the city's vibrant traditions and festivities. The Festa di San Nicola in May celebrates the city's patron saint with processions, music, and fireworks. The Settembre al Borgo festival showcases local arts, crafts, and performances, while the Bari International Film Festival attracts film enthusiasts from around the world.

Day Trips: Bari serves as an excellent base for day trips to nearby destinations in Puglia. Within a short distance, you can visit enchanting towns like Polignano a Mare, Alberobello with its iconic trulli houses, the beautiful seaside town of

Monopoli, or the charming city of Lecce, known

3.2 Lecce

Lecce, located in the southern region of Puglia, Italy, is a charming city known for its rich history, stunning architecture, and vibrant atmosphere. Here's a guide to help you explore Lecce and make the most of your visit:

Piazza del Duomo: Start your exploration in the heart of Lecce at Piazza del Duomo. This picturesque square is dominated by the magnificent Lecce Cathedral (Duomo di Lecce), an impressive Baroque masterpiece. Take some time to admire the intricate facade and step inside to explore its beautiful interior.

Basilica di Santa Croce: Just a short walk from the cathedral, you'll find the Basilica di Santa Croce. This church is a true gem of Lecce's Baroque architecture, with its ornate decorations and intricate carvings. Marvel at the intricacy of the stone work and explore the adjacent monastery.

Roman Amphitheatre: Lecce has a rich Roman heritage, and the Roman Amphitheatre is a testament to its ancient past. Located near Piazza Sant'Oronzo, this well-preserved amphitheater is a fascinating historical site. Take a stroll around the ruins and imagine the gladiator fights and performances that once took place here.

Piazza Sant'Oronzo: This lively square is named after the city's patron saint, Saint Orontius. It's a vibrant hub of activity, lined with cafes, restaurants, and shops. Admire the Roman column with a bronze statue of Saint Orontius on top and enjoy the lively atmosphere of the square.

Lecce's Historic Center: Explore the narrow, winding streets of Lecce's historic center (Centro Storico), known for its unique and intricate Baroque architecture. Admire the ornate balconies, detailed facades, and hidden courtyards as you wander through the streets. Don't miss the Porta Napoli, an impressive city gate that marks the entrance to the old town.

Palazzo dei Celestini: Visit the Palazzo dei Celestini, a former monastery turned museum. The building itself is a stunning example of Lecce's architectural style, and inside you'll find a collection of art and artifacts that showcase the city's history.

Piazza Sant'Oronzo Underground Museum: Beneath Piazza Sant'Oronzo lies a fascinating underground museum that offers a glimpse into Lecce's past. Explore the ancient Roman ruins, medieval artifacts, and archaeological finds that have been discovered in the city over the years.

Lecce's Cuisine: Indulge in the delicious local cuisine of Lecce. Sample some traditional dishes like "pasticciotto leccese," a sweet pastry filled with custard, and "orecchiette," a type of pasta typically served with local sauces. Explore the local trattorias and restaurants to savor the flavors of Puglia.

Beaches and Surrounding Areas: Lecce is also a great base for exploring the beautiful beaches and coastal areas of Puglia. Drive along the coast to visit stunning beaches like Punta Prosciutto or Porto Cesareo, or venture further to explore the charming towns of Otranto and Gallipoli.

Festivals and Events: Check if there are any festivals or events happening during your visit to Lecce. The city often hosts cultural events, music festivals, and religious celebrations that offer a unique and lively experience.

Remember to take your time to soak up the atmosphere, enjoy the local hospitality, and immerse yourself in the beauty of Lecce and its surroundings.

3.3 Alberobello

Alberobello, located in the picturesque region of Puglia, Italy, is a city that transports visitors to a fairytale-like world. Renowned for its unique architecture and enchanting atmosphere, Alberobello offers a one-of-a-kind experience that captures the essence of traditional Apulian life.

The most striking feature of Alberobello is its collection of trulli, traditional stone huts with conical roofs that dot the landscape. These iconic buildings, made entirely of limestone and without the use of mortar, give the city its distinctive appearance. Walking through the narrow streets lined with these whitewashed trulli is like stepping into a magical realm frozen in time.

As you explore Alberobello, you'll encounter two distinct districts: Rione Monti and Aia Piccola. Rione Monti is the larger and more famous of the two, with an abundance of trulli clustered together, creating a captivating labyrinth of alleyways. Here, you can wander through the narrow streets, marveling at the unique architecture and the decorative symbols painted on some of the trulli, representing religious, superstitious, or purely decorative motifs.

Within Rione Monti, you'll find the Trullo Sovrano, the only two-story trullo in Alberobello. This fascinating structure has been converted into a museum, allowing visitors to glimpse into the past and learn about the history and lifestyle of the region's inhabitants.

Aia Piccola, the smaller district, is just as charming, with its own collection of trulli and a more intimate atmosphere. Here, you can find local artisans selling handmade crafts and souvenirs, providing an opportunity to take a piece of Alberobello's magic home with you.

In addition to exploring the trulli districts, make sure to visit the Church of Saint Anthony of Padua, a beautiful church with a trullo-shaped facade. Inside, you'll discover ornate decorations and a peaceful ambiance.

To fully immerse yourself in the local culture, indulge in the delightful cuisine of Puglia. Alberobello boasts numerous restaurants and trattorias serving authentic Apulian dishes. From homemade pasta like orecchiette to the region's famous burrata cheese and fresh seafood, your taste buds are in for a treat.

If you have the time, venture beyond Alberobello to discover the wider Puglia region. Within a short drive, you can explore the coastal town of Polignano a Mare with its stunning cliffs and crystal-clear waters. Or head to the historic city of Lecce, known as the "Florence of the South," with its Baroque architecture and vibrant cultural scene.

Whether you spend a day or a few days in Alberobello, this enchanting city will captivate your heart and imagination. Its timeless charm, rich history, and warm hospitality make it a must-visit destination for anyone seeking a unique and unforgettable experience in Italy.

3.4 Ostuni

Nestled in the heart of the enchanting region of Puglia, in southern Italy, lies the picturesque town of Ostuni. Renowned as the "White City," Ostuni boasts a mesmerizing maze of whitewashed buildings that glisten under the warm Mediterranean sun. This ancient town is a true gem, offering visitors a glimpse into the rich history, vibrant culture, and stunning landscapes of the region.

One of the most captivating features of Ostuni is its striking architecture. As you wander through its narrow, winding streets, you'll find yourself surrounded by a sea of dazzling white buildings adorned with intricate balconies, ornate doorways, and charming flower pots. The town's whitewashed facades not only give it a unique and ethereal appearance but also serve a practical purpose, reflecting the sun's rays and keeping the interiors cool during the scorching summer months.

A visit to Ostuni wouldn't be complete without exploring its historic center, known as La Città Vecchia. Here, you'll discover a labyrinth of alleys and staircases that lead to hidden courtyards, quaint shops, and lively piazzas. At the heart of the old town stands the magnificent Ostuni Cathedral, an impressive example of Apulian Romanesque architecture. Step inside to admire its beautiful rose window, intricate frescoes, and soaring vaulted ceilings.

While strolling through Ostuni's streets, take the time to explore the local artisan boutiques, where you'll find unique handmade ceramics, intricate lacework, and traditional textiles. The town is also home to a bustling food market, where you can sample an array of local delicacies, including fresh olive oil, creamy burrata cheese, and fragrant orecchiette pasta. Be sure to indulge in the region's famous wines, such as Primitivo and Negroamaro, which perfectly complement the rich flavors of Puglian cuisine.

For panoramic views of Ostuni and its surrounding landscapes, make your way to the town's ancient defensive walls. From this vantage point, you'll be treated to breathtaking vistas of olive groves, vineyards, and the azure waters of the Adriatic Sea. As the sun sets, painting the sky in hues of gold and pink, the town transforms into a magical place, its whitewashed buildings glowing warmly in the twilight.

Beyond the town itself, Ostuni offers easy access to the stunning beaches of the Adriatic coastline. Just a short drive away, you'll find pristine stretches of sand and crystal-clear waters. Whether you prefer lounging on the beach, swimming in the refreshing sea, or partaking in water sports like windsurfing and sailing, the coastal areas near Ostuni provide a perfect retreat.

In addition to its natural and architectural beauty, Ostuni hosts a variety of cultural events and festivals throughout the year. From traditional processions and music concerts to food and wine fairs, there's always something happening in this vibrant town. The locals are known for their warm hospitality and love for their heritage, ensuring that visitors feel welcome and immersed in the authentic Puglian experience.

Whether you're a history buff, a nature lover, or simply seeking a tranquil escape, Ostuni has something to offer. With its enchanting ambiance, stunning architecture, and proximity to beautiful beaches, this captivating town in southern Italy promises an unforgettable exploration and an opportunity to immerse yourself in the beauty and charm of the White City.

3.5 Polignano a Mare

Polignano a Mare, located in the charming region of Puglia in southern Italy, is a picturesque coastal town that captivates visitors with its breathtaking beauty and rich history. Perched atop towering limestone cliffs overlooking the crystal-clear waters of the Adriatic Sea, Polignano a Mare offers a truly enchanting setting for exploration and discovery.

As you wander through the narrow, winding streets of the historic center, known as the "centro storico," you'll find yourself immersed in the town's authentic charm. The white-washed buildings adorned with colorful flower pots, the intricate balconies, and the ornate churches create a postcard-perfect scene at every turn. The town's unique architecture reflects a mix of influences from various civilizations that have left their mark on this ancient settlement.

One of the main attractions in Polignano a Mare is the breathtaking beach known as Lama Monachile or Cala Porto. This small, secluded beach is nestled between two cliffs, creating a dramatic and picturesque setting. The azure blue waters and the rugged cliffs make it a popular spot for sunbathing, swimming, and cliff diving. The sight of the crystal-clear sea contrasting with the rocky shoreline is simply awe-inspiring.

Exploring Polignano a Mare wouldn't be complete without indulging in its delectable cuisine. The town is renowned for its fresh seafood, and there's no shortage of fantastic seafood restaurants and trattorias serving up mouthwatering dishes. Be sure to try local specialties such as "riso patate e cozze" (rice, potatoes, and mussels) or "orecchiette alle cime di rapa" (ear-shaped pasta with turnip greens). Pair your meal with a glass of local wine, and you'll experience a true taste of Puglia.

For those with a keen interest in history and culture, Polignano a Mare has several noteworthy landmarks. The Church of Santa Maria Assunta, perched on the edge of a cliff, offers panoramic views of the Adriatic Sea. Inside, you'll find beautiful frescoes and a sense of tranquility. Another notable site is the Roman Bridge, an ancient structure that dates back to the 2nd century AD. Walking across this bridge, you'll be transported back in time and can imagine the bustling activity that once took place here.

In addition to its historical and natural attractions, Polignano a Mare is also a vibrant hub for arts and culture. The town has been a source of inspiration for many artists, poets, and musicians throughout the years. It hosts various cultural events and festivals, including the "Gusta Puglia" food and wine festival, which showcases the region's culinary delights.

Whether you're strolling along the cliffside promenade, savoring the local cuisine, or simply basking in the beauty of the town, Polignano a Mare offers an unforgettable experience. Its unique blend of history, natural beauty, and cultural richness make it a must-visit destination for anyone exploring the enchanting region of Puglia.

CHAPTER 4:UNFORGETTABLE LANDSCAPES AND BEACHES

4.1 Gargano Peninsula

The Gargano Peninsula, also known as Promontorio del Gargano, is a captivating landform located in the easternmost part of the Apulia region in southern Italy. Jutting out into the Adriatic Sea like a mighty promontory, this stunning coastal area is renowned for its exceptional beauty, diverse landscapes, and rich historical and cultural heritage.

Stretching over 70 kilometers, the Gargano Peninsula boasts an array of natural wonders. Its rugged cliffs and dramatic rocky formations, coupled with lush forests and charming coastal towns, create a picturesque setting that captivates visitors from all around the world. The region is often referred to as the "spur of Italy's boot" due to its distinct shape on the map.

One of the most striking features of the Gargano Peninsula is the Gargano National Park, established in 1991. This protected area covers a vast expanse of approximately 1,210 square kilometers, encompassing both land and marine environments. The park is home to a remarkable diversity of flora and fauna, including ancient olive groves, beech and oak forests, as well as rare species of orchids and carnivorous plants. Wildlife enthusiasts can spot numerous animal species, such as wildcats, foxes, deer, and a variety of bird species.

Within the Gargano National Park, the Foresta Umbra stands out as a particularly enchanting forest. Its name, which means "dark forest," derives from the thick canopy of trees that creates an almost mystical atmosphere. The Foresta Umbra is a paradise for hikers and nature lovers, with numerous trails leading through its ancient trees and offering breathtaking vistas along the way.

Apart from its natural beauty, the Gargano Peninsula is steeped in history and culture. The area has been inhabited since ancient times, and evidence of various civilizations can be found in the form of archaeological sites, cave dwellings, and medieval castles. Monte Sant'Angelo, a town perched high on the slopes of the Gargano, is particularly famous for its iconic Sanctuary of Monte Sant'Angelo, a UNESCO World Heritage site. This sacred place attracts pilgrims and tourists alike, who come to admire the impressive architecture and enjoy the panoramic views from its location.

Another notable town on the Gargano Peninsula is Vieste, known for its charming historic center and beautiful sandy beaches. With its whitewashed houses, narrow winding streets, and lively atmosphere, Vieste is a popular tourist destination. The town also serves as a gateway to the stunning sea caves and rock formations that dot the coastline, such as the Pizzomunno Rock and the Grotta dei Pipistrelli.

Visiting the Gargano Peninsula offers a unique experience that combines nature, history, and the warmth of Italian culture. Whether exploring its rugged landscapes, immersing oneself in the ancient forests, or basking in the sun on its pristine beaches, the Gargano Peninsula leaves an indelible mark on all who venture to this enchanting corner of Italy.

4.2 Salento Peninsula

The Salento Peninsula, located in the southernmost region of Apulia (Puglia) in Italy, is a captivating and picturesque area that offers a unique blend of natural beauty, rich history, and cultural charm. Jutting out into the Adriatic Sea, this slender strip of land is renowned for its stunning coastline, vibrant towns, traditional cuisine, and warm hospitality.

One of the defining features of the Salento Peninsula is its breathtaking coastline, characterized by crystal-clear turquoise waters, golden sandy beaches, and dramatic cliffs. The peninsula boasts some of the most beautiful beaches in Italy, attracting sun-seekers and water enthusiasts from all over the world. From popular tourist spots like Gallipoli, Otranto, and Santa Maria di Leuca to hidden gems like Porto Selvaggio and

Baia dei Turchi, the coastline offers a diverse range of beach experiences to suit every taste.

Beyond its stunning beaches, the Salento Peninsula is dotted with charming towns and villages that exude a distinct Mediterranean atmosphere. Lecce, known as the "Florence of the South," is the region's capital and a treasure trove of Baroque architecture. Its ornate churches, palaces, and piazzas adorned with intricate carvings and elegant façades showcase the rich cultural heritage of the area. Exploring the narrow alleys of Lecce's historic center, visitors can immerse themselves in the captivating ambiance and discover hidden gems at every turn.

The Salento Peninsula is also home to numerous small coastal towns and fishing villages that offer a glimpse into the traditional way of life in southern Italy. Gallipoli, perched on a rocky island connected to the mainland by a 16th-century bridge, is a popular destination that blends ancient history with modern attractions. Its charming old town, surrounded by fortified walls, is a maze of narrow streets, historic buildings, and lively squares where visitors can savor fresh seafood and immerse themselves in the vibrant local culture.

Otranto, another gem on the peninsula's eastern coast, boasts a stunning historic center that has been recognized as a UNESCO World Heritage site. Its ancient castle, mosaic-filled cathedral, and picturesque harbor make it a must-visit destination for history enthusiasts. Moreover, Otranto serves as the gateway to Salento's rugged and wild coast, known as the "Costa degli Altri," where visitors can explore breathtaking natural landscapes and hidden coves.

The culinary scene in the Salento Peninsula is a highlight in itself, offering a rich tapestry of flavors and traditions. The region's cuisine is deeply rooted in its agricultural heritage, with an emphasis on fresh, locally sourced ingredients. Visitors can indulge in delectable dishes such as orecchiette pasta with tomato and ricotta sauce, grilled octopus, burrata cheese, and taralli (traditional savory biscuits). Accompanying these culinary delights is the region's famous wine, especially the full-bodied red wines like Primitivo and Negroamaro, which are produced in the surrounding vineyards.

Whether it's exploring historic towns, lounging on pristine beaches, indulging in delicious cuisine, or simply soaking up the laid-back atmosphere, the Salento

Peninsula offers a truly unforgettable experience. Its combination of natural beauty, cultural heritage, and warm hospitality make it a destination that captures the hearts of all who visit.

4.3 Valle d'Itria

Valle d'Itria, also known as the Itria Valley, is a picturesque region located in the southern part of Italy's Apulia (Puglia) region. Nestled between the provinces of Bari, Brindisi, and Taranto, this enchanting valley is renowned for its charming countryside dotted with trulli, ancient olive groves, vineyards, and rolling hills.

The defining feature of Valle d'Itria is undoubtedly its trulli. These traditional dry stone huts with conical roofs are unique to this region and have become iconic symbols of Puglia. The trulli were originally built as agricultural dwellings, and their distinctive design, using prehistoric building techniques, has earned them UNESCO World Heritage status.

Alberobello, a town in the Itria Valley, is particularly famous for its concentration of trulli. Walking through the narrow streets of Alberobello's Rione Monti district feels like stepping into a fairytale village. The trulli, with their whitewashed walls and intricate stone decorations, create a magical atmosphere that attracts visitors from all over the world.

In addition to Alberobello, the Itria Valley is dotted with other charming towns and villages, each with its own unique character. Locorotondo, known for its circular historic center and its excellent white wines, is often considered one of the most beautiful villages in Italy. Cisternino, with its narrow streets and panoramic views, is another gem worth exploring. Ostuni, the "White City," sits on a hill overlooking the valley, showcasing a stunning ensemble of whitewashed buildings.

Apart from its architectural wonders, Valle d'Itria is also famous for its delicious cuisine. The region's fertile soil produces excellent olive oil, which is a key ingredient in many traditional dishes. Pugliese cuisine is known for its simplicity and emphasis on fresh, local ingredients. Pasta dishes like orecchiette with tomato sauce or with cime di rapa (turnip greens) are regional favorites. Other culinary highlights include succulent roasted meats, freshly caught seafood, and a wide array of cheeses and antipasti.

Exploring the countryside of Valle d'Itria is a delight for nature lovers. The rolling hills are adorned with ancient olive trees, some of which are centuries old. The olive groves produce some of Italy's finest olive oil, and many farms offer tours and tastings for visitors. The vineyards of the valley also produce excellent wines, especially the crisp white wines made from the Verdeca and Bianco d'Alessano grapes.

For those seeking outdoor activities, the Itria Valley offers plenty of opportunities for hiking, cycling, and horseback riding. The peaceful countryside, with its rural charm and breathtaking views, provides a tranquil escape from the hustle and bustle of city life.

In conclusion, Valle d'Itria is a captivating region in the heart of Puglia, Italy, characterized by its trulli, picturesque towns, delicious cuisine, and beautiful countryside. Whether you are drawn to its architectural wonders, culinary delights, or natural landscapes, the Itria Valley offers a truly unforgettable experience for travelers.

4.4 Trani

Trani is a picturesque coastal town located in the region of Puglia, Italy. With its rich history, charming architecture, and stunning seaside setting, Trani is a hidden gem that attracts visitors from all over the world.

One of the most striking features of Trani is its beautiful harbor, which has been a crucial center of maritime activity for centuries. The port is surrounded by historic buildings and offers breathtaking views of the Adriatic Sea. It's a great place to take a leisurely stroll, enjoy a coffee or gelato at one of the many cafes, or simply sit by the waterfront and watch the boats sail by.

Trani is renowned for its remarkable Romanesque cathedral, known as the Cathedral of San Nicola Pellegrino. This impressive structure dominates the city's skyline with its elegant white facade and rose window. Inside, visitors can marvel at the ornate sculptures, intricate mosaics, and the serene atmosphere that transports them back in time.

The town is also home to several other architectural gems, including the imposing Swabian Castle, which was built by Emperor Frederick II in the 13th century. The castle overlooks the sea and offers panoramic views of the coastline. It often hosts cultural events and exhibitions, allowing visitors to delve into Trani's fascinating past.

Trani's historic center, characterized by narrow cobblestone streets and whitewashed buildings, is a delight to explore on foot. As you wander through the alleys, you'll discover charming squares, hidden courtyards, and cozy trattorias serving up delicious local cuisine. Don't miss the opportunity to try some of Puglia's culinary specialties, such as orecchiette pasta, burrata cheese, and fresh seafood.

For those seeking a tranquil escape, Trani boasts several beautiful beaches where visitors can relax and soak up the sun. The sandy shores are ideal for swimming and sunbathing, and the clear waters provide a refreshing respite from the summer heat.

Beyond its natural and architectural wonders, Trani also hosts a vibrant cultural scene. The town often hosts music festivals, art exhibitions, and cultural events that showcase the region's rich heritage and contemporary creativity.

Trani's proximity to other notable destinations in Puglia, such as Bari and

Alberobello, makes it an excellent base for exploring the region. With its well-preserved historic center, stunning coastal scenery, and warm Mediterranean ambiance, Trani offers visitors a unique and memorable experience that captures the essence of Puglia's beauty and charm.

4.5 Santa Maria di Leuca

Santa Maria di Leuca, often referred to simply as Leuca, is a picturesque town located on the southernmost tip of the Salento peninsula in the Puglia region of Italy. It holds a special place in the hearts of locals and visitors alike due to its breathtaking natural beauty, rich history, and cultural significance.

One of the main attractions of Santa Maria di Leuca is its stunning coastline. The town is situated at the meeting point of the Adriatic and Ionian Seas, which creates a unique and captivating landscape. The crystal-clear turquoise waters, rugged cliffs, and hidden caves make it a paradise for nature lovers and photographers. The iconic Punta Ristola, a rocky promontory that marks the southernmost point of mainland Italy, offers panoramic views of the surrounding seascape and is a popular spot for tourists to admire the beauty of the area.

Santa Maria di Leuca is also known for its distinctive lighthouse, which stands tall at the tip of Punta Meliso. The lighthouse, built in the 19th century, serves as a guiding beacon for ships navigating the waters and adds to the town's charm. The panoramic viewpoint near the lighthouse provides visitors with an incredible vista, showcasing the meeting of the two seas and the picturesque coastline stretching into the horizon.

Apart from its natural attractions, Santa Maria di Leuca boasts a rich historical and cultural heritage. The town has been inhabited since ancient times and has witnessed the influence of various civilizations, including the Greeks,

Romans, Byzantines, and Normans. This cultural blend is evident in the architectural styles found throughout the town. Visitors can explore the elegant Liberty-style villas, ornate churches, and historic monuments that dot the streets of Leuca, showcasing the town's past and its significance as a crossroads of cultures.

The Sanctuary of Santa Maria de Finibus Terrae is a prominent religious site in Santa Maria di Leuca. Perched atop a hill overlooking the town, the sanctuary is dedicated to the Virgin Mary and attracts pilgrims from all over the region. Its impressive Byzantine-style architecture, adorned with intricate mosaics and frescoes, is a testament to the devotion and craftsmanship of the past.

Santa Maria di Leuca offers visitors a vibrant and lively atmosphere, especially during the summer months. The town comes alive with cultural events, festivals, and a bustling waterfront promenade where visitors can stroll along, enjoying the local cuisine, gelato, and souvenir shops. The combination of delicious seafood, fine wine, and the warm hospitality of the locals makes for a memorable experience.

In conclusion, Santa Maria di Leuca is a hidden gem in southern Italy that captivates visitors with its natural beauty, rich history, and cultural heritage. Whether you are seeking relaxation on pristine beaches, exploration of historical sites, or immersion in the local traditions, Leuca has something to offer to everyone. Its idyllic charm and the mesmerizing views at the tip of Italy's heel make it a must-visit destination for those looking to discover the beauty of Puglia.

CHAPTER 5: CULINARY DELIGHTS OF PUGLIA

5.1 Traditional Puglian Cuisine

The traditional cuisine of Puglia, also known as Apulian cuisine, is characterized by its simplicity, rustic flavors, and use of locally sourced ingredients. With a strong emphasis on olive oil, fresh vegetables, seafood, and pasta, Puglian cuisine offers a delightful culinary experience that reflects the region's agrarian roots and coastal influences.

One of the highlights of Puglian cuisine is the abundant use of extra virgin olive oil. Puglia is the largest producer of olive oil in Italy, and it plays a central role in almost every dish. The region's olive oil is known for its fruity and robust flavor, which enhances the taste of various dishes. Whether it's drizzled over salads, used for frying, or incorporated into sauces, Puglian olive oil adds a distinct character to the cuisine.

Vegetables are another essential component of Puglian cuisine. The region's fertile soil yields a wide variety of fresh and flavorful vegetables. Tomatoes, artichokes, fava beans, chicory, eggplants, peppers, and wild greens are commonly used in Puglian dishes. These vegetables form the base of many recipes, such as the classic Puglian pasta dish orecchiette con cime di rapa, which combines homemade pasta with broccoli rabe, garlic, and chili flakes, all sautéed in olive oil.

Puglia's long coastline provides an abundance of seafood, and it is celebrated in the regional cuisine. Fresh fish, shellfish, and mollusks take center stage in various preparations. Popular seafood dishes include frittura di paranza (mixed fried seafood), spaghetti alle vongole (spaghetti with clams), and pesce all'acqua pazza (fish poached in a flavorful broth). The simplicity of these dishes allows the natural flavors of the seafood to shine through.

Pasta holds a special place in Puglian cuisine, and the region is famous for its unique shapes and types of pasta. Orecchiette, a small ear-shaped pasta, is a

Puglian specialty and is often served with various sauces and toppings. Other regional pasta varieties include cavatelli, strozzapreti, and the long, thin pasta called chitarra. These pasta shapes are commonly paired with Puglia's fresh tomato sauces, often flavored with garlic, basil, and a generous drizzle of olive oil.

In addition to these main elements, Puglia boasts a variety of traditional baked goods and desserts. Taralli, small, crunchy bread rings flavored with fennel or black pepper, are a popular snack in the region. The pasticciotto is a sweet pastry filled with custard, typically enjoyed for breakfast or as a dessert. Another notable dessert is the cartellate, a type of fried pastry shaped like roses and drizzled with honey or vincotto (cooked wine reduction).

To accompany the flavors of the cuisine, Puglia offers a selection of local wines. The region is known for its robust red wines, such as Primitivo and Negroamaro, as well as crisp white wines like Fiano and Verdeca. These wines perfectly complement the rich flavors of Puglian dishes and showcase the region's viticultural heritage.

In summary, Puglian cuisine is a celebration of simplicity, quality ingredients, and traditional flavors. From the generous use of olive oil and fresh vegetables to the delectable seafood and unique pasta shapes, the cuisine of Puglia embodies the region's agricultural abundance and coastal charm. Exploring the traditional dishes of Puglia is a delightful journey into the heart of Italian culinary traditions.

5.2 Must-Try Dishes and Local Specialties

The region boasts a cuisine that is deeply rooted in its agricultural heritage, Mediterranean flavors, and fresh, local ingredients. Here are some must-try dishes and local specialties that you should not miss when visiting Puglia:

Orecchiette: One of the most iconic dishes of Puglia, orecchiette is a type of homemade pasta that resembles small ears (hence the name, which means "little ears" in Italian). It is typically served with a variety of sauces, but one of the most traditional and beloved is "orecchiette alle cime di rapa" (orecchiette with turnip greens). The pasta is cooked until al dente and tossed with sautéed turnip greens, garlic, chili flakes, and a drizzle of olive oil.

Burrata: Originating from the town of Andria in Puglia, burrata is a luscious and creamy cheese that is a must-try for cheese lovers. It is made from cow's milk and has a soft outer shell of mozzarella filled with a mixture of cream and cheese curds. When cut open, it releases a rich, buttery filling. Burrata is often served with ripe tomatoes, fresh basil, a sprinkle of salt, and a drizzle of extra virgin olive oil.

Taralli: These small, savory biscuits are a popular snack in Puglia. They are made from a dough of flour, olive oil, white wine, and salt, which is then shaped into small rings or twisted knots. Taralli can be flavored with various ingredients such as fennel seeds, black pepper, chili flakes, or even wine. They are often enjoyed with a glass of local wine or as part of an antipasto platter.

Focaccia Barese: Focaccia in Puglia takes on a unique and delicious form. Focaccia Barese is a fluffy and thick flatbread topped with cherry tomatoes, olives, and a generous drizzle of olive oil. It is baked until golden and crispy, and it's commonly enjoyed as a snack or as a part of a light meal.

Friselle: Friselle are twice-baked bread rings that are incredibly popular in Puglia, especially during the hot summer months. They are made from durum wheat flour and water, and after being baked once, they are soaked in water briefly to soften. Friselle are then topped with fresh tomatoes, basil, oregano, olive oil, salt, and sometimes with a sprinkling of oregano or dried chili flakes.

Fave e Cicorie: This simple yet satisfying dish combines two staple ingredients of Puglia: fava beans and chicory. The fava beans are boiled until tender and then mashed, creating a creamy texture. Chicory, a bitter leafy green vegetable, is sautéed with garlic and chili flakes. The two components are served together with a drizzle of olive oil and a sprinkle of salt. It's a delicious and hearty dish that reflects the region's rustic flavors.

When visiting Puglia, don't forget to try some of the local wines as well, such as Primitivo, Negroamaro, and Salice Salentino. These wines perfectly complement the rich and robust flavors of the local cuisine.

Exploring Puglia's culinary delights is a true feast for the senses. Whether you're savoring the pasta, cheese, bread, or vegetables, the region's dishes will leave a lasting impression and provide an authentic taste of Puglia's

5.3 Popular Puglian Wines

Puglian wine, also known as Apulian wine, has gained popularity worldwide for its distinctive flavors, rich history, and excellent quality. The region's favorable climate, fertile soil, and traditional winemaking techniques contribute to the unique character and diversity of Puglian wines.

Puglia benefits from a Mediterranean climate with long, hot summers and mild winters. This climate, along with the region's proximity to the Adriatic and Ionian Seas, provides the ideal conditions for cultivating grapes. The warm temperatures and ample sunshine allow the grapes to fully ripen, resulting in wines that are rich in flavor and aroma.

The fertile soil in Puglia is predominantly limestone and clay, with some areas featuring sandy or volcanic soils. This diversity in soil composition adds complexity to the wines produced in the region. The indigenous grape varieties thrive in these conditions, creating a wide range of wine styles.

One of the most well-known grape varieties from Puglia is Primitivo. This red grape is believed to be genetically identical to the Zinfandel grape from California. Primitivo produces robust, full-bodied red wines with rich fruit flavors of dark berries, cherries, and plums. These wines often have a velvety texture and a hint of spice, making them excellent choices for pairing with hearty dishes and grilled meats.

Negroamaro is another prominent grape variety in Puglia. It is responsible for producing red wines with a deep, intense color and a complex flavor profile. Negroamaro wines often exhibit notes of black fruits, such as blackberries and black cherries, along with hints of tobacco, licorice, and spices. They possess a good balance of acidity and tannins, making them suitable for aging.

Puglia is also known for its white wines, with the Trebbiano and Malvasia grape varieties being widely grown. These white wines tend to be crisp, refreshing, and aromatic, with flavors of citrus fruits, green apples, and floral notes. They are perfect for enjoying as an aperitif or pairing with seafood and light pasta dishes.

In recent years, Puglia has witnessed a renaissance in winemaking, with an emphasis on quality and innovation. Many producers are adopting modern techniques while respecting the region's winemaking traditions. This approach has led to the production of premium wines that showcase the unique terroir of Puglia.

Puglian wines are not only appreciated locally but have also gained international recognition. Their exceptional value for money, coupled with their distinctive flavors and versatility, has made them increasingly popular in the global wine market. Whether you are a red wine lover or prefer whites, Puglia offers a diverse range of options to satisfy any palate.

Exploring Puglian wines allows wine enthusiasts to discover the authentic flavors and expressions of this fascinating region. From rich and powerful reds to crisp and aromatic whites, Puglia's wines capture the essence of Southern Italy's winemaking heritage.

CHAPTER 6: CULTURAL AND HISTORICAL ATTRACTIONS

6.1 Castel del Monte

Castel del Monte, located in the region of Puglia, Italy, is a fascinating medieval fortress that stands as a testament to the architectural and historical richness of the area. This unique UNESCO World Heritage Site attracts visitors from around the world, drawing them in with its mysterious allure and intriguing design.

Situated atop a hill in the heart of the Apulian countryside, Castel del Monte is renowned for its octagonal shape, distinctive among European castles. Constructed in the 13th century by Emperor Frederick II, also known as Frederick II of Hohenstaufen, the castle embodies a blend of architectural styles, combining elements of Romanesque, Gothic, and Islamic influences.

The castle's octagonal shape is believed to symbolize the emperor's passion for the number eight, which he considered to be a perfect and harmonious number. Each of the castle's eight sides features an identical octagonal tower, creating a symmetrical and visually striking composition. The exterior walls are made of limestone, and the structure's compactness and austere lines add to its imposing presence.

Inside Castel del Monte, visitors can explore a series of rooms spread over two floors, featuring elegant arches, ornate fireplaces, and intricate decorations. The castle's interior showcases a mix of Christian and Muslim elements, including intricate mosaic floors, sculptures, and murals that highlight the diverse cultural influences present during Frederick II's reign.

The most notable room within the castle is the octagonal courtyard, where a well stands at its center. This open space serves as the focal point of the structure, and its purpose remains a subject of debate among historians. Some theories suggest it was used for gatherings, while others propose it had astronomical or symbolic significance. The true purpose of the courtyard remains shrouded in mystery, further adding to the allure and intrigue of Castel del Monte.

Beyond its architectural marvels, the castle also holds historical significance. It served as a hunting lodge, a royal residence, and even a prison throughout its long history. Despite periods of neglect and damage, Castel del Monte has been meticulously restored to its former glory, allowing visitors to experience its grandeur and gain insight into the region's medieval past.

The castle's location in the Puglia region provides additional charm. Puglia, also known as Apulia, is celebrated for its picturesque landscapes, olive groves, and charming towns. Visitors to Castel del Monte can also explore the surrounding countryside, taste the region's renowned cuisine, and enjoy the warm hospitality of the local people.

In conclusion, Castel del Monte in Puglia stands as a remarkable architectural gem, blending various influences from different eras and cultures. Its octagonal design, enigmatic history, and stunning location make it a must-visit destination for history enthusiasts, architecture lovers, and curious travelers seeking to unravel the mysteries of this medieval marvel.

6.2 Trulli of Alberobello

Alberobello, a small town located in the region of Puglia in southern Italy, is famous for its unique and enchanting trulli. These traditional limestone dwellings, with their conical roofs and whitewashed walls, create a picturesque and otherworldly landscape that has attracted travelers and explorers for decades.

Exploring the trulli of Alberobello is like stepping into a fairy tale. As you wander through the town, you'll find yourself surrounded by rows upon rows of these charming structures. Each trullo tells a story, with its distinct design and history etched into its very walls.

The origins of the trulli date back centuries, to a time when the region was under the rule of the Kingdom of Naples. The unique architectural style of the trulli can be attributed to a combination of factors, including the abundance of limestone in the area and the taxation system of the time. The trulli were built without mortar, using interlocking stones, creating a remarkable dry-stone construction technique that has stood the test of time.

Walking through the narrow streets, you'll encounter trulli of various sizes and shapes. Some are simple and humble, while others are adorned with intricate symbols and decorations. The roofs of the trulli are often adorned with pinnacle-shaped ornaments, adding to the whimsical charm of the town. Many trulli have been converted into shops, restaurants, and guesthouses, offering visitors a chance to experience the unique atmosphere firsthand.

One of the highlights of exploring the trulli is visiting the Trullo Sovrano, the only two-story trullo in Alberobello. This remarkable structure gives you a glimpse into the daily life of the past, with its furnished rooms and preserved artifacts. It's a fascinating step back in time, allowing you to imagine what it would have been like to live in a trullo centuries ago.

Beyond the trulli themselves, Alberobello is a place to immerse yourself in the local culture. The town's narrow streets are lined with small shops selling local crafts, souvenirs, and delicious regional products. You can sample the flavors of Puglia, from freshly baked bread to olive oil, wine, and traditional pastries.

For those interested in the history and craftsmanship behind the trulli, a visit to the Museo del Territorio is a must. This museum provides a comprehensive look at the construction techniques, tools, and daily life of the trullo builders. It's an opportunity to delve deeper into the rich heritage of this unique architectural style.

Exploring the trulli of Alberobello is a journey into a world of beauty, history, and tradition. It's a place where the past merges seamlessly with the present, creating a magical experience for visitors.

Whether you're strolling through the streets, savoring local delicacies, or simply admiring the architectural wonders, Alberobello and its trulli will leave an indelible mark on your memory, inviting you to return time and time again.

6.3 Historic Centers of Puglia Towns

Puglia is a land blessed with natural beauty, stunning coastlines, and a fascinating history. One of the most captivating aspects of this region is its historic centers, which offer a glimpse into the rich cultural heritage of Italy. From narrow cobblestone streets to ancient architectural marvels, exploring the historic centers of Puglia is an immersive experience that takes you on a journey through time.

One of the most renowned historic centers in Puglia is located in the city of Lecce. Often referred to as the "Florence of the South," Lecce boasts a remarkable display of Baroque architecture. Walking through the streets of Lecce's historic center, you'll be greeted by intricately carved stone facades, elegant palaces, and ornate churches. The centerpiece of the city, Piazza del Duomo, is home to the stunning Lecce Cathedral, a masterpiece of Baroque artistry. As you wander through the city's narrow alleys, you'll discover hidden courtyards, charming squares, and artisan workshops that showcase the city's rich artistic traditions.

Another gem of Puglia's historic centers is located in the city of Alberobello. This UNESCO World Heritage Site is renowned for its unique trulli houses, traditional dry stone huts with conical roofs. Walking through the streets of Alberobello feels like stepping into a fairy tale, as these iconic white-washed structures line the narrow lanes, creating a truly enchanting atmosphere. Exploring the interior of a trullo is a must-do experience, offering insights into the traditional way of life in Puglia.

Further south, the historic center of Ostuni, known as the "White City," offers a captivating blend of medieval charm and stunning panoramic views. Perched on a hilltop, the whitewashed buildings of Ostuni gleam under the Mediterranean sun, creating a striking contrast against the blue sky. The labyrinthine streets of the historic center are filled with picturesque alleys, archways, and hidden corners waiting to be discovered. Exploring Ostuni's historic center leads to breathtaking vistas overlooking the surrounding olive groves and the Adriatic Sea.

The city of Bari, Puglia's capital, is home to a vibrant historic center that combines medieval and modern elements. The narrow streets of the old town, known as Bari Vecchia, are a bustling maze of life, where you can witness the authentic daily routines of the locals. The Basilica of San

Nicola, an important pilgrimage site, stands as a magnificent example of Romanesque architecture. The atmospheric alleyways of Bari Vecchia also lead to charming squares, such as Piazza Mercantile and Piazza del Ferrarese, where you can savor traditional local delicacies in the vibrant outdoor cafés.

In addition to these cities, Puglia is dotted with countless smaller towns and villages that hold their own historic charm. Martina Franca, Locorotondo, and Cisternino are just a few examples of places where you can immerse yourself in the region's rich history and architecture. Each town boasts its unique character, with picturesque streets, ancient churches, and well-preserved historical buildings.

Exploring the historic centers of Puglia is like stepping into a living museum. It is a journey that takes you back in time, allowing you to appreciate the intricate craftsmanship, cultural traditions, and the vibrant stories woven into the fabric of these towns. Whether you're captivated by the Baroque beauty of Lecce, the fairytale-like trulli of Alberobello, or the medieval charm of Ostuni

6.4 Matera's Sassi

Exploring Matera's Sassi in Puglia is a captivating journey into the past, an immersive experience that takes you back in time to witness the architectural marvels and rich cultural heritage of this UNESCO World Heritage site. Matera, located in the southern region of Puglia, Italy, is renowned for its unique cave dwellings known as "Sassi."

The Sassi of Matera are a complex network of ancient cave dwellings, carved into the calcarenite rock formations that dominate the landscape. These dwellings, some of which date back to prehistoric times, were inhabited by generations of people who made ingenious use of the natural caves to create homes, churches, and even entire neighborhoods. The resulting cityscape is a remarkable blend of human ingenuity and harmonious integration with the natural environment.

As you stroll through the narrow, winding streets of the Sassi, you'll feel transported to another era. The architecture is a fusion of rustic simplicity and timeless elegance, with white stone facades and labyrinthine alleyways. The Sassi is divided into two main districts: Sasso Caveoso e Sasso Barisano. Each district has its own distinctive character and offers a glimpse into the different phases of Matera's history.

In Sasso Caveoso, you'll find the oldest cave dwellings, characterized by their irregular shapes and rough-hewn facades. The cave churches, such as the Church of San Pietro Caveoso and the Church of Santa Lucia alle Malve, are particularly noteworthy. These ancient places of worship feature Byzantine frescoes and provide a glimpse into the spiritual life of the community that once thrived here.

On the other hand, Sasso Barisano showcases a more refined architectural style. The cave houses in this district often have more regular shapes and elegant facades. Many of them have been converted into charming boutique hotels, restaurants, and artisan shops, allowing visitors to experience the unique atmosphere of Matera while enjoying modern comforts.

One of the highlights of exploring the Sassi is the opportunity to visit the Casa Grotta, a recreated cave dwelling that offers a glimpse into the daily lives of Matera's inhabitants in the past. Inside, you'll find original furniture, tools, and household items that provide insight into the way of life in this ancient settlement.

Beyond the architectural wonders, Matera's Sassi offers a wealth of cultural experiences. The city has become a vibrant hub for art, culture, and gastronomy. Numerous art galleries, craft workshops, and cultural festivals celebrate the artistic heritage of the region. Matera was also designated as the European Capital of Culture in 2019, further solidifying its status as a cultural destination.

Additionally, the local cuisine is a delight for food enthusiasts. Traditional dishes showcase the rich flavors of the region, with specialties such as orecchiette pasta, caciocavallo cheese, and hearty meat dishes. Exploring the Sassi also means indulging in the local cuisine, with numerous charming trattorias and restaurants offering authentic Puglian fare.

To make the most of your visit, consider taking a guided tour or joining a walking tour led by knowledgeable local guides. They can provide valuable insights into the history, architecture, and culture of the Sassi, ensuring you don't miss any hidden gems.

Exploring Matera's Sassi in Puglia is an unforgettable experience that offers a unique perspective on human history and resilience. It is a testament to the power of human creativity and adaptability, as well as a reminder of the importance of preserving our cultural heritage.

6.5 Puglian Folklore And Festivals

Puglia, a charming region in southern Italy, is not only renowned for its stunning landscapes and delicious cuisine but also for its rich folklore and vibrant festivals. Steeped in history and tradition, Puglia offers a captivating glimpse into the ancient customs and cultural heritage of the region. From colorful processions to lively music and dance, exploring Puglia folklore and festivals is an immersive experience that will leave you enchanted.

One of the most celebrated festivals in Puglia is the Festa di San Nicola, which takes place in the city of Bari in early May. This festival is dedicated to Saint Nicholas, the patron saint of Bari and the inspiration for the modern-day Santa Claus. The festivities include religious processions, where a statue of the saint is carried through the streets, accompanied by traditional music and prayers. The city comes alive with vibrant decorations, street performances, and delicious local delicacies. It's a joyous event that brings together locals and visitors alike to honor this beloved saint.

Another notable festival in Puglia is the Cavalcata di Sant'Oronzo, celebrated in the city of Lecce on August 26th. This festival commemorates the city's patron saint, Sant'Oronzo, and showcases the cultural heritage of Lecce. The highlight of the festival is the spectacular horse parade, where beautifully adorned horses and riders take to the streets, captivating the spectators. The procession is accompanied by traditional music, and the air is filled with a festive atmosphere. During the festival, the city also hosts concerts, exhibitions, and street performances, making it a lively and enchanting experience.

Puglia is also known for its vibrant folk dances, and the Taranta Dance Festival is a testament to this rich tradition. This music and dance festival celebrates the ancient folk dance called the "pizzica tarantata," which has its roots in the belief that the bite of a tarantula spider could be cured through frenzied dancing. The festival, held in various towns across Puglia during the summer months, features live performances by renowned musicians and dancers, inviting everyone to join in the energetic and infectious dance. It's a mesmerizing experience that immerses you in the region's folklore and traditions.

Aside from these major festivals, Puglia is dotted with smaller, yet equally captivating, local celebrations throughout the year. From religious processions during Easter to grape harvest festivals in the autumn, there is always something to discover in this culturally rich region. These festivals offer a unique opportunity to witness traditional costumes, hear ancient dialects, taste traditional foods, and participate in age-old rituals.

When exploring Puglia folklore and festivals, it is also worth venturing into the smaller towns and villages, where local traditions are deeply rooted. These communities often organize their own events and festivities, showcasing their unique customs and folklore. Whether it's the colorful "cucù" masks of Barletta or the traditional "Tarantella" dance in Molfetta, each town has its own distinct folklore waiting to be explored.

In conclusion, exploring Puglia folklore and festivals is an immersive journey into the rich cultural heritage of the region. From the religious processions to the lively music and dance, these celebrations offer a glimpse into the ancient traditions and customs that have shaped Puglia's identity. Whether you're captivated by the horse parades of Lecce or the energetic Taranta dance, these festivals provide an unforgettable experience that will leave you with a deeper appreciation for Puglia's vibrant folklore.

CHAPTER 7: OUTDOOR ACTIVITIES AND NATURAL PARKS

7.1 Hiking And Nature Trails

Hiking and exploring nature trails in Puglia is an excellent way to immerse yourself in the region's beauty and discover its hidden gems. From coastal paths to rural countryside trails, Puglia offers a wide range of outdoor activities for nature enthusiasts.

One of the most renowned hiking destinations in Puglia is the Gargano National Park. Situated on the Gargano Peninsula, this park showcases a unique combination of lush forests, rugged cliffs, and stunning coastal vistas. The Sentiero

Italia, a long-distance hiking trail that spans the entire country, passes through the Gargano National Park, providing hikers with an opportunity to explore its scenic wonders. Along the way, you can discover ancient caves, picturesque villages, and breathtaking viewpoints overlooking the Adriatic Sea.

Another remarkable hiking experience can be found in the Itria Valley, famous for its distinctive cone-shaped trulli houses. This picturesque countryside region offers a network of trails that wind through olive groves, vineyards, and rolling hills. One of the most popular routes is the Valle d'Itria Trail, which takes you through charming villages like Alberobello, Locorotondo, and Martina Franca. The trail allows you to admire the unique architecture of the trulli and enjoy the peaceful ambiance of rural Puglia.

For those seeking coastal beauty, the Salento Peninsula offers stunning hiking opportunities. The Porto Selvaggio Natural Park, located near Nardò, is a true paradise for nature lovers. The park features a coastal trail that meanders through Mediterranean maquis vegetation, leading to hidden coves, pristine beaches, and crystal-clear waters. Exploring this trail allows you to admire the unspoiled beauty of the Salento coastline and revel in the tranquility of nature.

Puglia is also home to the Alta Murgia National Park, a vast area characterized by rolling hills, karst formations, and ancient rock settlements. This park provides a variety of hiking routes that allow you to immerse yourself in the region's rich history and natural splendor. The trails in Alta Murgia will take you through ancient ruins, such as the Castel del Monte, a UNESCO World Heritage site, as well as through vast expanses of wildflowers and grazing fields where you can spot local wildlife.

When embarking on hiking and nature trail activities in Puglia, it is essential to be prepared with proper hiking gear, including sturdy footwear, a map or GPS device, and sufficient water and snacks. Additionally, respecting the environment and following any guidelines or regulations set by the park authorities is crucial to preserve the natural beauty of these areas.

Whether you choose to explore the coastal paths, rural countryside trails, or national parks, hiking and nature trails in Puglia offer a wonderful opportunity to connect with nature, soak in the region's rich heritage, and create unforgettable memories of this beautiful part of Italy.

7.2 Water Sports And Beach Activities

Puglia is known for its stunning coastline along the Adriatic and Ionian Seas. With its crystal-clear waters, golden sandy beaches, and beautiful coastal landscapes, Puglia offers a paradise for water sports enthusiasts and beach lovers alike. From thrilling adventures to relaxing beach activities, Puglia has something to offer for everyone.

One of the most popular water sports in Puglia is windsurfing. With its consistent wind conditions, the region attracts windsurfers from all over the world. The coastal towns of Taranto, Brindisi, and Otranto are particularly famous for windsurfing, offering ideal spots for both beginners and experienced riders. Whether you want to glide along the waves or perform tricks on the water,

Puglia's windsurfing scene won't disappoint.

Another thrilling water sport to try in Puglia is kitesurfing. With its strong winds and long stretches of sandy beaches, Puglia provides excellent conditions for this adrenaline-pumping activity. The towns of Santa Maria al Bagno, Porto Cesareo, and Torre Lapillo are known for their kitesurfing schools and rental facilities, making it easy for visitors to get started or improve their skills. Feel the rush as you harness the power of the wind and glide across the water, propelled by a colorful kite.

For those seeking a more relaxed water activity, paddleboarding is an excellent option. Puglia's calm waters and picturesque coastline make it an ideal place to explore on a paddleboard. Whether you choose to paddle along the shores of Polignano a Mare, Gallipoli, or Santa Maria di Leuca, you'll be treated to breathtaking views and a peaceful atmosphere. Paddleboarding is also a fantastic way to discover hidden coves, caves, and secluded beaches that can't be accessed by land.

Of course, Puglia's beaches themselves offer plenty of opportunities for relaxation and enjoyment. The region boasts numerous pristine sandy beaches, many of which are awarded Blue Flag status for their cleanliness and quality. From the renowned beaches of Polignano a Mare and Pescoluse to the lesser-known gems like Porto Selvaggio and Baia dei Turchi, Puglia's coastline offers a diverse range of options for beachgoers.

Apart from swimming and sunbathing, beach volleyball and beach soccer are popular activities on Puglia's shores.

Many beaches have designated areas where visitors can join friendly matches or tournaments, creating a lively and energetic atmosphere. Additionally, beach yoga and meditation sessions are often organized, allowing participants to find inner peace while surrounded by the calming sound of the waves.

In conclusion, Puglia offers a plethora of water sports and beach activities that cater to various interests and preferences. Whether you're seeking thrilling adventures like windsurfing and kitesurfing, or you prefer a more relaxed experience such as paddleboarding or simply enjoying the sun-soaked beaches, Puglia's coastal region is a haven for water sports enthusiasts and beach lovers alike. So pack your swimsuit, grab your gear, and get ready to dive into the beauty of Puglia's water sports and beach activities.

7.3 Grotto Exploration

Grotto exploration in Puglia, Italy, offers a fascinating journey into the region's underground wonders. Beneath the surface lies a hidden world of caves and grottos that captivate the imagination of adventurers and nature enthusiasts.

Puglia's grottoes are the result of centuries of geological processes, shaping intricate formations and unique underground landscapes. The region is famous for its karst topography, characterized by soluble rocks such as limestone and dolomite that have been eroded over time, creating caves, sinkholes, and underground rivers.

One of the most renowned destinations for grotto exploration in Puglia is the Grotte di Castellana. Located near the town of Castellana Grotte, these caves are a mesmerizing natural wonder. The Castellana Caves stretch for about 3 kilometers and consist of a network of chambers, tunnels, and stalactite-studded galleries. Exploring this underground labyrinth provides an awe-inspiring experience, as visitors traverse narrow passages and encounter breathtaking rock formations that have formed over thousands of years.

Another notable grotto in Puglia is the Grotta Zinzulusa, situated along the Adriatic coast near Castro. Accessible both by land and sea, this cave is famous for its stunning stalactites and stalagmites that create a surreal environment. The grotto derives its name from the "zinzuli," the local term for bats, as these fascinating creatures inhabit the cave's darker corners.

In addition to these prominent caves, Puglia is dotted with numerous smaller grottoes and sea caves that offer their own enchantment. Along the coastline, visitors can embark on boat tours to explore sea caves, such as the Grotta della Poesia near Roca Vecchia. This natural pool, surrounded by cliffs, provides a refreshing swimming experience and a glimpse into the region's ancient history, as archaeological finds have revealed human presence in the area dating back thousands of years.

Grotto exploration in Puglia is not just an opportunity to witness natural wonders but also a chance to delve into the region's history and cultural heritage. Many caves have served as shelters for prehistoric humans, and archaeological discoveries within these grottoes have provided valuable insights into early civilizations. Exploring the caves offers a sense of connection with the past and an appreciation for the geological and anthropological significance of the region.

Whether you are an adventurer, a nature lover, or a history enthusiast, grotto exploration in Puglia promises a memorable and immersive experience. The combination of awe-inspiring landscapes, geological wonders, and cultural heritage makes it an extraordinary destination for those seeking to uncover the hidden treasures beneath the surface of this beautiful Italian region.

7.4 Wildlife And Birdwatching

Puglia offers fantastic opportunities for wildlife and bird watching enthusiasts to explore and observe a wide variety of species in their natural habitats.

Puglia's diverse ecosystems include coastal areas, wetlands, forests, and countryside, each harboring unique wildlife populations. The region is a critical stopover point for migratory birds, making it an ideal destination for birdwatching. Here are some of the notable wildlife and bird watching activities you can enjoy in Puglia:

Gargano National Park: Situated on the Gargano Peninsula, this national park is a haven for nature lovers. Its varied terrain, consisting of forests, coastal cliffs, and wetlands, supports a rich array of flora and fauna. Gargano is particularly famous for birdwatching, with species such as peregrine falcons, golden eagles, and hoopoes gracing the skies. The park also offers guided tours and educational programs to enhance your wildlife experience.

Saline di Margherita di Savoia: This coastal wetland in the north of Puglia is a vital habitat for migratory birds, especially during the spring and autumn seasons. Flamingos, herons, egrets, and numerous other waterfowl can be spotted here. Visitors can explore the area on foot or by bike along designated trails and observation points.

Alimini Lakes: Located near Otranto, the Alimini Lakes are a system of two freshwater lakes surrounded by lush vegetation. The lakes and their surrounding areas are home to a variety of bird species, including kingfishers, grebes, and various ducks. You can explore the lakeside paths and rent boats or kayaks for a closer look at the avian inhabitants.

Bosco delle Pianelle: This forested area near the town of Cisternino offers a peaceful retreat for nature enthusiasts. The forest is home to a diverse range of bird species, including woodpeckers, owls, and various songbirds. Guided tours and birdwatching walks are available to help visitors spot and identify the different species.

Torre Guaceto Nature Reserve: Located along the Adriatic coast, this protected area encompasses a wide range of habitats, including sand dunes, wetlands, and Mediterranean scrubland. The reserve attracts a plethora of bird species, including gulls, terns, and migratory birds such as storks and herons. Visitors can explore the reserve's trails, join guided tours, or even participate in bird ringing activities.

When engaging in wildlife and bird watching activities in Puglia, it is crucial to respect the natural environment and follow ethical guidelines. Keep a safe distance from the animals, avoid disturbing their habitats, and refrain from feeding or touching them. Binoculars, field guides, and knowledgeable local guides can enhance your experience and help you identify and appreciate the region's fascinating birdlife.

Puglia's diverse landscapes and abundant wildlife make it a captivating destination for wildlife enthusiasts and bird watchers alike. Whether you're a seasoned birder or a novice nature lover, exploring the region's natural treasures is sure to leave you with unforgettable memories of the region's flora and fauna.

CHAPTER 8: PRACTICAL INFORMATION AND TRAVEL TIPS

8.1 Accommodation Options

The region of Puglia has many different accommodation options for travelers including villas, apartments, bed and breakfasts, hotels, and campsites.

Vacation villas in Puglia are popular amongst visitors for those who want to have a private and luxurious experience while in Puglia. These villas offer a wide array of amenities and services such as onsite swimming pools, lush gardens, and private views. Many villas are located in rural areas where visitors can sample traditional Italian culture and enjoy a more secluded escape.

Apartments in Puglia are another great option for travelers who are looking for a more independent accommodation experience. These apartments range from affordable small studios to luxury venues. Puglia apartments are generally within walking distance of major tourist attractions and amenities.

Bed and breakfasts in Puglia are a popular option for visitors seeking a homemade experience while in Puglia. B&Bs usually offer daily breakfast and dinner, as well as a variety of activities. Guests at B&Bs can also benefit from the owners' local knowledge, which can make traveling in Puglia much more enjoyable and easier to navigate.

Hotels in Puglia offer a variety of services and amenities and are available in both urban and rural locations. Hotels in Puglia typically offer a mix of traditional Italian hospitality and classic European designs.

Finally, camping in Puglia is available as well, offering visitors an additional affordable option. Many campsites are located in rural areas near the coast, offering guests access to stunning shorelines and natural parks.

8.2 Local Transportation

Puglia is located in the southeastern region of Italy and is known for its delicious cuisine, beautiful beaches, historic towns, and picturesque landscapes. As such, the region is visited by tourists from all over the world. When traveling to Puglia, visitors will find that the local transportation is well-developed and convenient.

Public buses are the most popular form of transport in Puglia. Regional Trenitalia operates a comprehensive network of routes across all of Puglia, linking its towns and cities. The fares are very affordable and reliable. For those traveling further afield within the region, there are Intercity buses which travel between cities, towns, and villages, often connecting to other regions.

Ferries are another option for travelers who are looking to travel to the smaller islands or coasts of Puglia. Ferries depart from the main port cities of Bari and Brindisi and the larger islands such as Salento, Tremiti, and the Tremiti Islands.

For those looking to travel around Puglia in a more independent way, cars, cycles, and motor scooters can be rented in many cities and towns. This is a great way to explore the smaller towns and countryside, although you should be aware of local road rules and regulations.

Finally, there are the trains which link cities and larger towns. The network is run by Ferrovie dello Stato, an Italian rail company. There are also international connections to other parts of Italy, as well as to other European countries.

In short, the local transportation in Puglia is reliable and convenient. Whether you're traveling by bus, ferry, car, train, bicycle or scooter, getting around the region has never been easier.

8.3 Safety And Emergency Contacts

Puglia is a region in Italy that is known for its pristine beaches, Mediterranean climate and plethora of cultural activities. Safety is a primary concern for all travelers and visitors to this region, and the Italian government takes measures to ensure that all people are safe from harm.

In Puglia, the Polizia di Stato, Carabinieri and Guardia di Finanza are the three police forces that are responsible for maintaining the safety and security of the region. These forces are adept at handling criminal cases, medical emergencies, and civil disturbances. In addition, the Italian fire brigade, the Vigili del Fuoco, is available for emergency calls related to fires and other disasters.

In addition to the police services in Puglia, there are a number of other emergency contacts available in the area. These include the Italian Red Cross, the Italian Coast Guard, and the Italian Civil Protection Service. All of these services are available 24/7 and can be reached in case of an emergency.

The Italian Coast Guard can also be reached if a boat is involved in a search and rescue operation, or for any other marine-related emergencies. The Italian Civil Protection Service can be contacted if an urban crisis needs to be resolved, or if natural disasters have occurred.

With regards to safety, visitors should also take note of the various signs and regulations that are in place to ensure a safe stay in Puglia. These include speed limits, street parking regulations, and beach safety protocols.

It is important to remember to, whether traveling to Puglia or any other location, stay up to date on safety protocols. Be sure to consult with local authorities and familiarize yourself with the local emergency contacts in case of an emergency or serious incident.

8.4 Language And Communication

Puglia is a Mediterranean region in southern Italy that is known for its diverse population and its strong cultural heritage. The dominant language spoken in Puglia is Italian, but other languages such as Greek, Albanian, Spanish, Croatian, French and German are also spoken by certain communities living within the region. In addition, many dialects of Italian are spoken throughout the region, the most dominant being Salentino, Tarentino and Barese.

Communications in Puglia are quite diverse. Most people use a combination of oral and written communication, supported by modern forms of technology such as smartphones and computers. Of course, many Puglieses prefer to communicate through traditional means, and this is reflected in their daily interactions with each other. In businesses and other professional contexts, the Italian language is generally used, though dialects may also be used depending on the specific context.

Overall, language and communications in Puglia play an important role in the cultural continuity of the region. It is used to facilitate interactions between different ethnic and racial groups, and to maintain the strong cultural identity of the region.

CHAPTER 9: PUGLIA'S HIDDEN GEMS AND OFF THE BEATEN-PATH

9.1 Lesser-Known Towns and Villages

Despite its popularity, there are many lesser-known and lesser-visited towns and villages in Puglia that are worth exploring.

Ostuni is a small and picturesque hilltop town located in the region of Apulia. It is most famous for its well-preserved architecture which includes churches, towers and gates. The town is a great example of medieval Italian architecture, and visitors can explore the old town with its narrow cobbled streets and white-washed houses. Another must-see in

Ostuni is the Cathedral of Santa Maria Assunta and the bell tower made out of local limestone.

Grottaglie is a tranquil town known for its pottery and ceramics. It is home to the Ceramics Museum, where visitors can learn about the history of the craft and admire the diverse range of products. It is also known for its excellent olive oil and gastronomy.

Nicotera is a small fishing village located in the Salento area. It is the ideal destination for visitors who appreciate tranquility and relaxation. Visitors will find stunning scenery of the Maritsima coast and a variety of amenities including historical sites, restaurants and bars.

Sternatia is a small village located in the province of Lecce with archaeological roots dating back to the 4th century BC.

It is the perfect destination for an Italian history and culture trip. Visitors to Sternatia can explore and enjoy the rural environment, traditional architecture and cultural heritage - especially its food!

Galatina is another ancient village with an attractive old town. It is famous for its religious significance and it is home to several iconic churches. The Sanctuary of Santa Croce and the Church of Santa Lucia are particularly noteworthy.

San Pietro Vernotico is a small village situated in between the Adriatic and Ionian Seas. Visitors can explore the traditional narrow streets of the old-town and discover its gastronomy which is based on seafood and local products. It is a great spot to spend a day away from the crowds and relax in the lovely setting.

If you are looking for an off-the-beaten path destination in Italy, then these lesser known towns and villages in Puglia are definitely worth a visit. Whether you want to explore the architectural heritage, enjoy the local culture and gastronomy, or just relax on the beach, Puglia has something for everyone.

9.2 Secret Beaches And Coves

Puglia is the perfect place for your Mediterranean getaway. It's dotted with secret beaches and coves just waiting to be explored. And if you want a truly unique experience, Puglia offers plenty of secret spots, hidden away from the hustle and bustle of the crowds. Whether you want to spend an overnight stay or just spend the day relaxing in the sun, these beaches and coves in Puglia have you covered.

Take a boat ride to Granelli Beach - a small bay tucked away in the rocky outcrops of Salento. Granelli is perfect for picnics, sunbathing, and swimming, and offers some of the most amazing views of the Apulian sea.

Take your getaway further south to Calenella Beach in Porto Cesareo. This secret beach offers various amenities, making it the perfect place to relax and unwind. You can explore crystal-clear waters and find secluded spots to soak up the sun in privacy.

Make a stop at Castro Marina, where you'll find two hidden gems - Malva Beach and Tremiti Beach. These stunning beaches feature golden sands and tranquil waters, making them the perfect spot for a romantic getaway. For a more active day, bring your snorkeling gear and explore the deep waters filled with exotic marine life.

Ugento Beach in Porto Giunco is the ultimate secret cove. With its secluded nature, jagged rocks, and shallow beaches, this is an ideal spot for those wanting to enjoy a peaceful beach day. With crystal-clear waters and plenty of nearby hiking and biking trails, you'll feel like you're in another world.

If you're searching for a spot away from it all, check out the many secret beaches and coves in Puglia. Whether you're looking for a beach getaway with a group or a romantic escape for two, these hidden gems are sure to exceed expectations.

9.3 Rural Masserie And Farm Stays

Masserie and farm stays in Puglia offer visitors the chance to experience Italy's most idyllic countryside. Amidst sprawling fields and ancient olive trees lies a treasure trove of farmhouses, rural villas and rustic masserie (farmhouses). These accommodation options provide visitors with a unique and authentic experience, away from the hustle and bustle of the major cities of southern Italy.

Masserie are traditional farming establishments located in the southeastern Italian region of Puglia. Found atop hills and nestled among olive groves, the walled buildings have been a mainstay of the region for centuries. Boasting beautifully styled interiors typical of southern Italian décor, many masserie come with a private swimming pool and often beautiful views of the Mediterranean coastline.

For those looking to get closer to nature and explore the countryside while enjoying some of the best food in Italy, farm stays in Puglia provide the perfect opportunity. From learning how to cook a traditional Puglian dish, or wander the olive groves and vineyards in search of produce, you can immerse yourself in the rich culture of the region.

These countryside retreats also often feature a range of activities such as horse riding, walking and cycling tours, hot air balloon rides, and wine-tasting and food-sampling sessions, giving you an opportunity to explore the region in more depth and learn about its past and traditions.

At masserie and farm stays throughout Puglia, you can treat yourself to the unique atmosphere that centuries of peasant life have created. From relaxing sunny days spent lounging by a pool, learning about the local cuisine, and discovering the beauty of the Puglian countryside, a holiday on a masseria or farm stay in Puglia will be an unforgettable experience.

9.4 Day Trips And Excursions From Puglia

There are many exciting day trips and excursions to be had from Puglia, perfect for those seeking to explore southern Italy.

The city of Matera is less than two hours away from Puglia. Matera was made famous by the popular film "The Passion of the Christ", and is known for its unique "Sassi" caves, troglodyte houses built within the cliffside, and the beautiful cathedral of San Pietro Caveoso.

Another popular day trip from Puglia is to the nearby town of Alberobello. This unique town is home to the trulli houses, cone-shaped dwellings constructed with white stone and features a distinctive peak of bricks.

Visitors to Puglia may also wish to take a day trip to the Salento region, located on the "heel" of the Italian boot. This region features stunning beaches, historical monuments, and the beautiful town of Lecce.

Sarajevo is another great day trip from Puglia. Located just three hours away, Sarajevo is a vibrant city filled with culture and history. Visitors here can take in the city's mosques, bazaars, and pubs, as well as explore some of the city's famous sites including the Sarajevo National Museum and Sarajevo Cathedral.

No visit to Puglia would be complete without a visit to the nearby city of Bari. Here, visitors can explore the old town, sample the delicious seafood, and enjoy the traditional puppet show, "Taranta".

Finally, visitors to Puglia may wish to take a boat ride to the beautiful island of Tremiti, located just off the coast. Known for its crystal clear waters and stunning sunsets, the Tremiti Islands are the ideal destination for a day trip away from the hustle and bustle of mainland life.

CHAPTER 10: USEFUL PHRASES AND VOCABULARY

10.1 Basic Italian Phrases

Here are some basic Italian phrases that can be helpful for beginners:

Ciao! - Hello! (informal)
Buongiorno! - Good morning!

Buonasera! - Good evening!

Buonanotte! - Good night!

Grazie! - Thank you!

Prego! - You're welcome!

Mi chiamo... - My name is...

Come ti chiami? - What's your name? (informal)

Come si chiama? - What's your name? (formal)

Dove abiti? - Where do you live?

Mi dispiace. - I'm sorry.

Per favore. - Please.

Mi scusi. - Excuse me. (formal)

Scusa. - Excuse me. (informal)

Non capisco. - I don't understand.

Parla inglese? - Do you speak English?

Mi piace molto! - I like it a lot!

Mi piacerebbe... - I would like...

Quanto costa? - How much does it cost?

Dove si trova...? - Where is...?

Che ora è? - What time is it?

Posso avere il conto? - Can I have the bill?

Mi aiuti, per favore? - Can you help me, please?
Mi scusi, dove si trova il bagno? - Excuse me, where is the bathroom?
Buon viaggio! - Have a good trip!

These are just a few basic phrases, but they should come in handy when interacting with Italians or navigating through Italy. Remember to practice pronunciation and intonation to communicate effectively in Italian.

10.2 Local Dialects And Expressions

Puglia has its own unique local dialects and expressions. Here are some examples:

Barese Dialect:

"Mènne" or "Maivé" - Meaning "mine" or "my goodness," used to express surprise or disbelief.

"Farauàggh" - Equivalent to "What are you doing?" or "What's going on?"

"Fischiatèmm" - Let's go! It's an expression used to encourage someone to hurry up.

"Jè" - Yes, used as a confirmation or agreement.

"Cciù" - Goodbye or see you later.

"Spimàtt" - A playful way of saying "wait a moment" or "hold on."

Salentino dialect:

"Scusaj" - Excuse me or pardon.

"Li canne" - Literally meaning "the dogs," it's used as an expression of surprise or disbelief.

"Stè' 'uorte" - Stay strong, a phrase of encouragement.

"'Nciucare" - To eat or have a meal.

"Bpuméte" - Fantastic or amazing.

"Stu jurnu" - Today.

Tarantino dialect:

"Qué chiste?" - What's going on? Used to ask about someone's situation or news.

"St'à votà" - It's raining.

"Paccalité" - To be afraid or scared.

"Mònne" - Let's go or come on.

"Stu pede" - This guy. Used to refer to someone, often with a negative connotation.

"'Ndamène" - Come with me or let's go together.

Please note that these are just a few examples, and there are many more dialects and expressions within Puglia. The dialects can vary even within different towns or villages in the region.

10.3 Food And Drink Vocabulary

Here is a selection of food and drink vocabulary that you might encounter when exploring the gastronomic delights of Puglia:

Antipasto: The Italian term for appetizer, typically consisting of a variety of cured meats, cheeses, olives, and marinated vegetables. In Puglia, antipasti often include local specialties like burrata cheese and taralli (crunchy, ring-shaped breadsticks).

Orecchiette: A type of pasta that is popular in Puglia, characterized by its round, concave shape resembling a small ear. Orecchiette is often served with traditional Pugliese sauces, such as ragù (meat sauce) or broccoli rabe.

Frisella: A round, dried bread roll that is a staple in Puglia. Frisella is typically soaked in water or olive oil to soften it before being topped with fresh tomatoes, olive oil, and salt. It is a popular summer dish in the region.

Focaccia: A flatbread that is a beloved specialty in Puglia. Pugliese focaccia is often topped with cherry tomatoes, olives, oregano, and a drizzle of olive oil. It can be enjoyed as a snack or as part of a meal.

Burrata: A luscious, creamy cheese that originated in Puglia. Burrata is made from mozzarella and cream, giving it a soft, buttery texture. It is often served with fresh tomatoes and basil, drizzled with olive oil.

Polpo: Italian for octopus, polpo is a popular seafood ingredient in Pugliese cuisine. Grilled or stewed, it is often seasoned with garlic, parsley, and olive oil, resulting in tender and flavorful dishes.

Taralli: Small, crunchy breadsticks that are a staple snack in Puglia. They are often flavored with fennel seeds, black pepper, or olive oil. Taralli come in various shapes and sizes, and they can be sweet or savory.

Primitivo: A red wine grape variety that is indigenous to Puglia. Primitivo wines are known for their rich, full-bodied flavors and often exhibit notes of blackberry, plum, and spice. They are a perfect pairing for Pugliese cuisine.

Negroamaro: Another important red wine grape variety grown in Puglia. Negroamaro wines are known for their dark color, robust character, and flavors of black fruit, chocolate, and herbs. They are often enjoyed with hearty meat dishes.

Pasticciotto: A delicious pastry originating from the town of Lecce in xPuglia. Pasticciotto consists of a shortcrust pastry shell filled with a rich, creamy custard. It is a popular dessert and breakfast treat in the region.

These are just a few examples of the food and drink vocabulary you might encounter when exploring the culinary delights of Puglia. The region's cuisine is diverse and offers a wide range of flavors and specialties that showcase the freshest ingredients and the rich cultural heritage of the area.

10.4 Getting Around Vocabulary

When it comes to getting around in Puglia, language barriers can sometimes pose a challenge. While Italian is the official language spoken in the country, and thus in Puglia as well, it's not uncommon to encounter situations where English or other languages may not be widely understood. However, with a bit of preparation and some handy tools, you can navigate through Puglia and make your way around even if you don't speak the local language fluently. Here are a few strategies to help you get around:

Learn some basic Italian phrases: Before visiting Puglia, it's helpful to learn a few key phrases and expressions in Italian. Simple greetings, numbers, directions, and common phrases like "Please" (per favore) and "Thank you" (grazie) can go a long way in establishing a basic level of communication with locals.

Utilize translation apps: In this digital age, translation apps are a traveler's best friend. Install a reliable translation app on your smartphone, such as Google Translate or Microsoft Translator, which can provide real-time translations of words, phrases, and even sentences. These apps often have an offline mode, allowing you to download language packs in advance and use them without an internet connection.

Carry a pocket dictionary or phrasebook: Although it may seem old-fashioned, having a pocket dictionary or phrasebook can come in handy when you encounter language barriers. Look for one specifically focused on travel phrases and basic vocabulary. You can quickly look up words or phrases you need and show them to locals if necessary.

Use visual aids: When language fails, visual aids can save the day. Carry a map or use navigation apps to help you find your way around the region. Pointing to locations or using hand gestures can also be effective in conveying your message. Additionally, having a photo or screenshot of your intended destination can help you communicate with taxi drivers or ask for directions more easily.

Seek assistance from locals or tourist information centers: The people of Puglia are known for their warmth and hospitality. Don't hesitate to approach locals for help or guidance. Many will try their best to understand you or find someone who can assist you. If you're in a tourist area, look for tourist information centers where staff members are accustomed to dealing with visitors and can provide guidance in multiple languages.

Join guided tours or hire local guides: Participating in guided tours or hiring local guides can alleviate the language barrier and ensure a smoother experience. Tour guides are typically fluent in multiple languages and can provide valuable insights into the region's history, culture, and attractions.

Remember, a positive attitude and a willingness to communicate and connect with locals will go a long way. Even if you don't speak the same language fluently, a friendly smile and a respectful demeanor can bridge gaps and make your time in Puglia enjoyable and rewarding.

CONCLUSION

Puglia Map

Puglia, also known as Apulia in English, is a region located in southern Italy.

When examining a map of Puglia, you'll notice several key features:

Geography: Puglia is primarily a coastal region, with a long coastline stretching over 800 kilometers (500 miles). The region is bordered by the Adriatic Sea to the east and the Ionian Sea to the southeast. The landscape is characterized by rolling hills, fertile plains, and picturesque countryside.

Provinces: Puglia is divided into six provinces: Bari, Brindisi, Foggia, Lecce, Taranto, and Barletta-Andria-Trani.

These provinces are further divided into numerous municipalities and towns.

Major Cities and Towns: Bari, the capital of the region, is the most populous city and serves as a transportation hub. Other notable cities include Lecce, known as the "Florence of the South" due to its stunning Baroque architecture, and Brindisi, a historic port city. Other charming towns worth exploring include Alberobello with its unique trulli houses, Ostuni with its whitewashed buildings, and Gallipoli with its beautiful beaches.

National Parks and Nature Reserves: Puglia is home to several protected areas, including Gargano National Park in the northern part of the region. This park encompasses a rugged promontory with cliffs, forests, and sandy beaches. Other notable natural areas include the Foresta

Umbra, the Salento coast, and the marine protected areas along the coastline.

Transportation: Puglia is well-connected by transportation networks. The region has several airports, with Bari Karol Wojtyła Airport being the largest and busiest. The region also has a well-developed railway system, allowing for easy travel within Puglia and connections to other parts of Italy.

Points of Interest: Puglia is known for its historic and cultural attractions. Some must-visit sites include the UNESCO World Heritage Site of Alberobello, the trulli houses of Valle d'Itria, the Romanesque architecture in Bari's Old Town, the Baroque city center of Lecce, and the stunning beaches of the Salento Peninsula.

Overall, a map of Puglia showcases the diverse landscapes, charming towns, and cultural treasures that make this region a popular destination for tourists seeking both natural beauty and historical richness.

Made in the USA
Middletown, DE
29 October 2023

41562471R00109